Hearing God

7 Practices to Listen Better, Hear More, and
Get Stronger in the Faith

Hearing God

7 Practices to Listen Better, Hear More, and
Get Stronger in the Faith

Tanya Logan

Finch Hollow
PRESS

Finch Hollow Press Florida, USA

Finch Hollow
PRESS

Index

Welcome!

I am an author, blogger, and artist. I specialize in helping Christians improve their walk with God by removing distractions. I am also a wife and mother. I love bicycle riding, swimming, gardening, traveling, and creating. Most of all, I love connecting with people like you who want to grow their faith.

The information I'm going to share with you in this book is what I have learned over time through personal experience like leading Bible studies, earning a bachelor's degree and a master's degree in Christian Education, and being employed in various church positions over the past 25 years.

But more importantly, I am just like you. I struggle. I am broken. I don't always have the answer, despite my formal training and many years of personal experience.

I continue to grow and learn, and you will to. But the most important thing is to get started. So – let's begin!

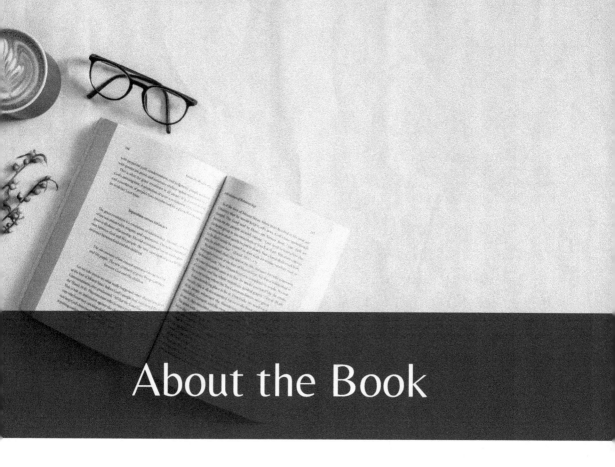

About the Book

This book, or course as I prefer to think of it, will help you to focus on ways that you can get closer to God by listening for his voice. It will not attempt to change your beliefs, your denomination affiliation, or how you attend church. This is only about you and your relationship with God.

There are a few links to audio and video portions of the course inside this book. Please don't skip over those; they're a part of the lesson structure (and you paid for them). I've used varied formats in part to mix it up to make it interesting, and partly because people have different learning styles so some may prefer the audio. The links are also given at https://biblestudyplanet.com/hearing-god-links.

Myself, I am a visual learner. I like to read, and I like to have steps laid out for me –which is why I've outlined steps for you. Each section contains several steps to follow. You don't have to do them in the order they're written. It is only a suggestion. Likewise, you might choose to skip over some sections and focus more on others. This too is okay. Your journey is yours and yours alone, so use this course as it best suits where you are right now.

Many of the links you will see lead you to free articles, websites, audios, or videos. Some of the links are to other resources, like books I particularly find useful or courses that have helped me along the way. You don't have to buy any of them, and I don't suggest that you do right now, but you may find that they are helpful to you in the future.

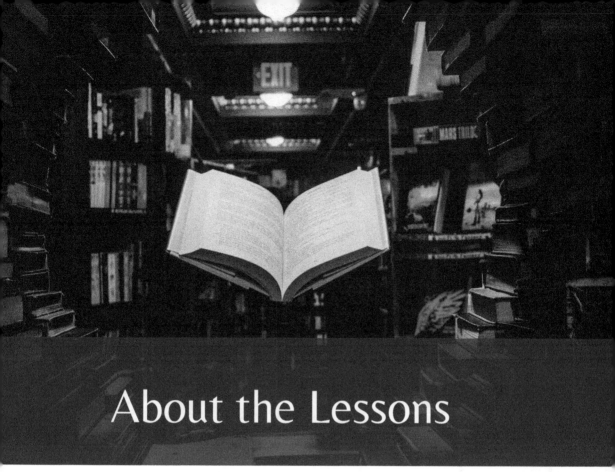

About the Lessons

The recorded webinars and audios were mostly created specifically for this course. But some of them were already recorded and so you might hear things that aren't relevant to this. It's okay; just ignore it. The videos are all located on YouTube @BibleStudyPlanet

I am aware that I use the word "you" far too much, so sometimes I resort to using "the reader" or people, Christians, God's people, etc. interchangeably. Yet - I want you to feel as if I'm talking one-on-one with you, so please don't feel put off if the words I'm using are not quite as personal or, conversely, if it's a little too intimate.

The end of each lesson will have a "To Do and To Be" section, which is a bullet list of your assignments. They're all suggestions, not commands. It's simply a summary of what you learned in the lesson.

If you have any questions at all, feel free to e-mail me at tanyawriter@gmail.com.

A Sacred Space

I'am so glad you have chosen to take this journey! This course will help you to:

- ➲ Find a sacred space

- ➲ Develop a routine for prayer

- ➲ Try a discipline you haven't tried before

- ➲ Begin to journal the journey

- ➲ Listen with your heart

- ➲ Get the Word in front of you more than once a day

- ➲ Find practical ways to practice love, holiness, and humility

> 66
> ———
>
> If Man Is Not Made For God, Why Is He Only Happy In God?
>
> Blaise Pascal

You may not choose to do all of these things, but they are available for you to study.

The course lessons are straightforward and direct, and will give you the simplest information for getting started. You may choose to continue on your journey with more specific teachings later. For now, I recommend that you do not search the Internet or read other information about these steps. In this way you can focus deeply on the lessons included here. Later, you can go deeper. I have included some links and Bible verses for that.

By spending some time on a single phase of the journey, you will give each step the attention it deserves. Sometimes people jump from one source of information to another, and they never manage to implement what they learn. Your relationship with God is the most important relationship you have had or will ever have. So we want to deepen your focus as much as possible. Learning to focus or "go deeper" in this way is key to forming the relationship you want with the Lord. There will always be different things and new approaches that you want to try. For now, let's stick to this one approach.

Your story is beautiful and important. Most of all, it is yours and yours alone. God did not make anyone else like you. You are entirely unique. If loving the Lord with all your heart, soul, and might is what you want, don't let one more thing get in your way.

A Place To Call Your Own

——————— ...

One of the most important parts of your life with God is having a place you consider sacred. This does not have to be an entire room, but it may need to be somewhere other than a busy messy desk or a room where the kids play.

Luke 5:16 says, "But Jesus often withdrew two lonely places and prayed." (NIV)

In order to emulate Jesus, then, we need a 'lonely' place where we can pray. A place to withdraw from the world. When my three children were growing up, I didn't have any space to devote to prayer except a small kidney-shaped desk in the very front of the house. It was located right beside the front door and at first I couldn't see how in the world this busy space could allow me to have devotions. But I cleaned out its four small drawers and laid the important things on the desktop: a Bible, pens and highlighters, and a candle. Every time I went to pray, I lit the candle. I used the desk only for Bible study, prayer and devotion time.

66

———

Am I only a God nearby," declares the Lord, "and not a God far away? Who can hide in secret places so that I cannot see them? Do not I fill heaven and earth? Jeremiah 23:23, 24

I found over time that the little desk became a sacred space. It did not matter what was going on around me; sitting at the desk was like an oasis in the storm.

Now the children are grown and gone, and we have recently downsized. My little prayer desk went with one of the kids. My big desk is used for writing. But in my bedroom is my grandmother's rocking chair. My grandmother was a very godly woman and I'm sure many prayers and much Bible reading went on in that space. I am continuing the tradition by using the rocking chair for my own sacred space. Often you will find me on my knees in front of the chair.

You don't have to have a special place; you can pray in every situation throughout any part of your day. You can pray at lunch, while waiting in line, and while driving. Many people pray while walking for exercise each day. But for true intercessory or "deep" prayer, I feel a need for a consecrated place. Maybe you could move the furniture around to accommodate it. Some families even have an altar built especially for kneeling and prayer.

If you cannot find a place to pray inside your home, consider outdoors. This depends on your weather, of course. I live in Southwest Florida and have a screened lanai on the back of the house with plenty of seating. Sometimes I go out there for prayer time. Other times, I sit on our dock. Perhaps you have a bench under a tree, or a low wall to sit by and pray. Rick Warren has a Prayer Garden. Habakkuk had a watchtower.

If you cannot find a place to pray inside, consider going outdoors.

If none of these work for you, a church might be a sacred space you can use for prayer. Many times through the week, churches are quiet. Yours might find a small chapel or other space you could call your own for prayer time. The purpose in finding a place to pray isn't about the place. By utilizing a certain location, these things will happen:

- ⊃ You will begin to go there regularly
- ⊃ It will begin to beckon you to come and pray
- ⊃ It will become sacred

Going Deeper

Let the words of my mouth and the meditation of my heart be acceptable unto you, my Lord my strength, and my redeemer.
Psalm 19:14

Read Matthew 6:5-6 from The Message:

Here's what I want you to do: Find a quiet, secluded place so you won't be tempted to role-play before God. Just be there as simply and honestly as you can manage. The focus will shift from you to God, and you will begin to sense his grace.

Meeting with God

...

Sometimes it's that time, according to the clock, and we simply aren't in the right frame of mind to meet with God. At least, that's how it feels. I find it's best to go ahead and call on him anyway when this happens.

For one thing, you never know when you're going to have a chance encounter with someone who doesn't know Him. More specifically, someone who doesn't know Him, but would like to. that's when we know the appointment was God-ordained!

Wouldn't you hate to arrive at that divine appointment and realize you weren't quite ready?

You can't say hey God, just give me 15 more minutes; or hey, could you come back later? I'm not ready for this encounter yet .

Chances are if you've been spending your daily *prayer* time at your little spot, your timing will be just exactly as God wanted. Your words will be ordained; your witness well - taken.

Thank you Lord , that you always equip us in the way we should go.

To Do and to Be

Outfit your space as it suits you. Some ideas:

- a special Bible
- pens
- highlighters
- bookmarks
- candles
- a cup of coffee
- a good reading light,
- a soft cushion to sit on
- a blanket for your lap.

Notes

Become aware of the sacredness

Use your new space to meet with God.

Notes

Prayer as a Routine

I'd like to say that prayer comes naturally, that it is easy to remember and of course I pray every moment of every day. It wouldn't be true. It is easy to get to the end of the day and say whoops, I didn't pray again today. Incredibly easy. So I find that the best way to make sure I do connect with God daily is by creating a routine. Maybe you feel this way, too.

It is important to have a routine anyway; routines help us be sure we did everything we needed to do before we left the house. Routines make sure we don't skip the deodorant or forget to feed the dog. Routines ensure that the house gets cleaned and picked up as

Prayer does not fit us for the greater work -Prayer is the greater work
Oswald Chambers

needed. So it makes sense to connect with the Lord of the universe as a part of our routine. Intentional prayer time, if you will.

Many people pray first thing in the morning. If you know me well, you know that is my least favorite time of day. If I prayed in the morning, there is no telling what I might say! Or whether I'd fall asleep in the middle. Even the names wouldn't be coherent as I read them from my prayer journal.

So instead, I pray a little bit later. It's still morning, but I've given myself a half-hour for coffee and an hour of cleaning or practicing piano. By the time I meet with the Lord, it is 10 or 11 AM but I have my wits about me.

You may be different. You might get children off to school, rush to work, rush home and cook dinner, and finally find yourself free at 8 PM. So your time could be eight or nine o'clock in the evening. It doesn't matter what time you choose; what is important is that we are starting a routine.

Someone once said that some people act like praying first thing in the morning is "the only" time to do it –that it's a sin to pray sometime other than 5 AM. Please do not fall for this; that's simply what works best for those people. God is waiting on us no matter what time of day it might be. He created us for his companionship. That means he wants us to show up-- not that he is asking us to give him a particular hour.

At first, you may need to set an alarm to remind you that it is time to pray. Someone told me that setting a clock for prayer time was getting too legalistic, so I tried it. I found it to be a really nice way to ensure that I prayed every day. Rather than being legalistic, it felt freeing to me.

Anyway, you are only doing it for a short while to help you get into a routine. You could also write it into your appointment book, guaranteeing that you will remember.

Another way to remind yourself to pray is to tie it to another activity. This is what I taught my music students to do with their practice; they tied it to another routine. So they might always practice piano after dinner, or practice violin right after playing video games.

I personally don't recommend prayer during other activities at this point in our journey. That's just me. Studies show we only do one thing well at a time , and I want my prayer time to be totally focused on God. So for this part of your routine, please do not pray while driving or exercising, but give it its own special time in your sacred space. Remember that our overall goal is to hear from God, so we want to make Him our primary focus. For now, you do not need to specify a minimum or maximum time to spend on prayer. Prayer brings you closer to God, and it doesn't matter how much time you spend in it. What matters is the commitment. Be as willing to pray as you are to eat each day.

Should You Read the Bible Before You Pray?

...

It is good to have one's mind set on God before praying. It is not necessary to read from the Bible, but it does seem to lead us closer to the relationship we want. Please note that in Lesson 6, we will go over Knowing Scripture and talk more about getting into the Bible daily. You might start with a short devotional reading or a daily Bible reading. I have an ambitious reading schedule on my website for the New Testament https://biblestudyplanet.com/bible-study-plans, or you can do an Internet search on "daily Bible reading" and find tons. Look at how much reading there is and be sure it works with your schedule. By having a reading plan, you skip over the part where you have to figure out what to read. That keeps you from being ambivalent and not reading at all!

To Do and to Be

Be at your appointed space at the appointed time.

Assemble the items you need. Light your candle, if you choose to have one. Consciously invoke your five senses.

Speak from your heart. Speak as if God is your closest, most trusted friend – because he is! No subject is too small, and no topic should be left uncovered. Remember the prayers of people in the Bible like Moses, Elijah, and Jeremiah, these are people who prayed honestly and openly. God rewarded them for their openness.

When you have said what you want to say, listen for the voice of the Holy Spirit. Sit quietly, and listen as long as you think you should.

Become aware of the sacredness

Use your new space to meet with God.

Notes

The prayer of a righteous man is powerful and effective.

Going Deeper

———— ...

Choose a bigger, important prayer time that will be your annual prayer time. Mark it on your calendar. It might be during Lent, New Year's Day, or another significant date. Schedule a period of time, anywhere from 4 to 24 hours for your personal prayer retreat. Get alone, just you and God, and spend that time listening to his voice through Scripture reading and prayer.

Write the date of your planned prayer journey here.

What Happens When We Pray?

——— ...

It is an awesome privilege to have an audience with our loving God. Just think, you cannot get an appointment with your doctor or a leading government official.

Sometimes you can't even get face time with your local pastor. Yet, begin to pray and you will immediately be face to face with the one person who truly has power. It's nothing short of amazing.

Please listen to the YouTube recording, What Happens When We Pray. located at https://youtu.be/IoLQixJECGM Record your thoughts below.

Notes

Trying out a Spiritual Practice

To some people, spiritual disciplines are a little scary. Depending on your age, you might think they're old-fashioned or that spiritual disciplines are too New Age for Christian folks. But the definition of discipline can mean practice, method or process. So a spiritual discipline is merely a process for practicing your divine habits.

That process might be a method of prayer, worship, or reflection. It might be a season of abstinence from things like talking, food, or Sabbath activities. There are many ways to practice faith that can lead to growth.

> Prayer does not fit us for the greater work -Prayer is the greater work
> Oswald Chambers

Describing all of the practices would take a whole book, so for the purposes of this course I will mention a few and you can choose from among them. I encourage you to simply choose the first one that resonates with you, rather than analyzing.

PRACTICE	PURPOSE
Bible study	To come to know the Bible deeply and understand its place in my life
Self-examination	To open myself to scrutiny and surrender the faults I recognize to Jesus for the purpose of becoming transformed
Centering Prayer	To be aware of God's presence with a still spirit
Humility	To be like Jesus; giving up power in order to be more loving and kind
Meditation	To look deeply into the meaning of God's word
Prayer walking	To practice intercessory prayer with Jesus while walking in particular places

There are many other spiritual disciplines; if this list does not include something new or appealing to you, please email me at tanyawriter@gmail.com and we will find one you would like to try.

My Spiritual Practice

...

In the following pages we will look at each of the Spiritual Practices in more detail. Feel free to look through these pages to see which one is calling to you.

We do not earn favor from God by doing, so these disciplines will not serve us that way. Instead, they help us face the Holy Spirit, letting him show us how to move into the rhythm of life that Christ aches to teach us.

Change can be difficult. In *Spiritual Disciplines Handbook*, the author says, "Keeping company with Jesus in the space between wanting to change and not being able to change through effort alone can be a difficult thing to do."[1]

Plan to set aside about a half hour each day for working on your spiritual discipline. Some may take more or less time, of course. Keep a record of what you did and how you felt about it.

Write your chosen spiritual practice here

---

[1]   Ahlberg, Adele, Spiritual Disciplines Handbook: Practices that Transform Us, Loc 213 Kindle.

Bible Study as a Spiritual Discipline

...

If you've been trying to get back into your Bible lately, it might make sense for "Bible study" to be your discipline of choice for the week.

Studying the Bible has many benefits, including forming the basis for the other disciplines. God in His infinite grace gave us this written record, which he breathed out. Reading it draws us to the Holy Spirit, who then guides us.

Reading the Bible is like fuel; it helps you know what to pray for, it enriches your own life, and it makes you hunger for more of God. Jesus said, "It is written: Man must not live on bread alone but on every word that comes from the mouth of God."[2]

For this course, since you are probably spending only one week on your discipline, you might pick just one book of the Bible to study. You can choose one that speaks to you, or one that you find more difficult if you like a challenge!

Part of the reason people don't read their Bibles consistently is that they choose a big selection and then try to rush through reading it; the reading becomes a task, just another mark on the to-do list. To avoid this problem, choose a smaller amount of reading and be ready to possibly hear from the Lord and spend time praying, crying, singing, or Just being in His presence.

Bible Scholars intensely observe and question; that's what makes them good students. Most use three basic steps:

1	Observe -what does it say?
2	Interpret – what did it mean to the original hearers?
3	Apply – how does it apply to me in this day/age?

BOOK OF THE BIBLE

1.   Read the entire book through, preferably aloud.

See if you can identify the 5 Ws and H: Who, What, Where, When, Why, How.

2.   2nd Reading. Write down the main idea and the structure of the book.

Use note cards or paper. By structure I mean is it poetry, narrative, an epistle?

How is the book arranged or divided?

If you didn't answer all your 5 Ws+H, continue to answer those.

3.   Now make observations as you read it a 3rd time.

What is the same? What key phrases are repeated? Use different colored pencils to mark who is speaking, who he is speaking to, and key phrases. I usually copy the page from my Bible and use the copy for markup. Here is the system I use:

Blue is the writer of the book.

Orange is who he's writing to.

God, Jesus, and the Holy spirit are yellow.

Purple is for positive repetitious phrases.

Brown is for sin or sin behavior.

Those are my own. Feel free to make your own or follow someone else's. Precept Ministries has the most well-known, in-depth system of marking but I found it was pulling me away from the meaning, so I stopped using it. You can see a good example of their system in this post.

4.   Fourth reading. Write a summary of your observations.

5.   Interpretation

What did this mean in its original context? For this you may need to turn to an outside source, like a Bible dictionary or other book. A public library is a great resource for these. If you do not have access to any of those, an online search may turn up just what you need.

6.   Application

Can you find any timeless truths (truths that apply to both people at the time it was written and today)? Write them out. How do those truths apply today? Are they more applicable in your personal life, education, or to the church as a whole?

Self-examination as a Spiritual Practice

...

Self-examination is a chance to look at your own choices, attitudes, and thought processes and see how they work for you or against you. The way you self-examine might be a practice of praying, worshiping, or reflecting. It might be a season of abstinence from things like talking, food, or Sabbath. activities. There are many ways to practice faith that can lead to growth.

There are many ways to practice self-examination. Some focus on level of consciousness, or how we find God. Others look for sin in order to put themselves aright with God. Some take that to an extreme – and that's what we want to avoid.

A man ought to examine himself before he eats of the bread and drinks of the cup.
1 Corinthians 11:28 (NIV)

There is a fine line between acknowledging your true responsibility in a situation, and in beating yourself up for every minor infraction. To that end, the self-examination or Examen, is not meant to be a downer.

The beauty about God is he's on your side. he doesn't want you beating yourself up any more than I do! Especially if you're already beaten down, from someone, something, or just "life".

So be sure to include the attitude of gratitude, the joy in your heart, and some plain old simple loving God because he's God. Ok?.

The Examen shouldn't give you a feeling of futility. It is a beautiful thing, a way to checklist yourself and see if you could be lacking in some way, and most of all to look toward tomorrow as a gift.

A true knowledge of ourselves cannot be acquired without diligent and frequent self-examination. To this duty there exists in human nature a strong repugnance, so that by most it is greatly neglected. But when it is attempted, we are in much danger of being misled by self-love and prejudice.

To acquire any true knowledge of ourselves a good degree of honesty and impartiality is essentially requisite. But an honest desire to arrive at the truth is not the only prerequisite to self-knowledge: the mind must be enlightened in regard to the standard of rectitude to which we ought to be conformed: the Word of God should dwell richly in us, and by its principles and precepts we must form all sentiments respecting ourselves.

Arthur Pink.[3]

3   Pink, Arthur. Studies in the Scriptures, Vol. 7. Sovereign Grace Publishers, 2005.

Learning to Self-Examine

———   ...

Let's take the Examen practice and utilize it only once each day. I suggest using it at the end of the day.

Settle yourself in your prayer area or another quiet, uninterrupted space. Consider each of the 5 steps:

1. Allow yourself to become aware of God's presence.

2. With gratitude, review your day.

3. Listen to your emotions. Be aware of the changes in them as you think through the day.

4. Choose one part of the day and pray about it.

5. Look forward to tomorrow.

Ask God to forgive each sin as it comes to mind. If you need a checklist, you might use the 10 Commandments:

- ⮫ Have no other Gods: Did I neglect to put God first? Have I neglected prayer?

- ⮫ Have no idols: What have I put first? Have I participated in ungodly things like astrology, fortune-telling and the like? Am I my own idol?

- ⮫ Do not take the Lord's name in vain: Have I used God's name as a bad word? Have I treated things lightly that ought to be treated with reverence?

- ⮫ Write each sin on paper (you can tear it up later) and look them over. Ask: Is there a pattern?

- ⮫ Do I repeat certain sins over and over? If so – you're normal, for this is usually the case.

- ⮫ Are there sins on the list that hurt others? The idea that sins do not hurt others is dangerous. Even small sins are damaging. Remember, God hates all sin.

- ⮫ Do you need to confess in the presence of others? If so, arrange appropriate steps.

Ask God for future guidance in overcoming sin. It is only by His grace and the cross of Jesus that we are forgiven. "Create in me a pure heart, O God, and renew a steadfast spirit within me." (Psalm 51:10)

01 Forgive yourself. As you think deeply on your personal way of sinning, remember that God already forgave you, so there is no point in carrying around a heavy burden of guilt. If we do not forgive ourselves, then we must ask whether we truly trusted God to "throw it in the sea of forgetfulness."

02 Tear up your paper or burn it.

Experience the joy that follows.

Centering Prayer as a Spiritual Practice

...

Centering prayer is merely another tool for having a conversation with God. It is not meant to take the place of any other prayer, rather it is intended to help you focus more on your communication.

In centering prayer, you are moving beyond using words to simply resting in God's presence, much as you would lean back against your father's knees when you were little. Remember when you did that, how you just sat with him? Words were not necessary. Your father was probably looking down at you and assessing what you needed - were you hungry? Thirsty? And maybe he'd pat your head or your shoulder. But you were just enjoying being with your dad.

That's exactly what centering prayer feels like, at least for me. It's coming into his presence and spending time together. It's not something most of us are accustomed to, so it may take a little time before you can stay focused and that's okay.

The Lord is near to all who call on him, to all who call on him in truth. He fulfills the desire of those who fear him; He also hears their cry and saves them.
1 Corinthians 11:28 (NIV)

Some people like to choose a word or phrase to use. If they find themselves drifting, they re-center themselves using that word. Like "Jesus," or "Come Holy Spirit." You have the choice to have a special word, or not.

Following is a short worksheet for how to practice centering prayer. Remember that this is your chosen practice, please do this daily for one week. You might want to copy the next page 5 times.

Don't forget to journal about it! This is something that changed rapidly and divinely.

Centering Prayer Worksheet

01 Find a word to use for your prayer that describes God and who he is.

02 Meditate on this word for several minutes.

03 Sit in silence, waiting on God. Do not feel that you need to accomplish anything. You aren't required to speak, ask questions, or look for answers. Simply be.

04 If your thoughts turn away, gently return them to your waiting state.

Humility as a Spiritual Practice

Humility does not come easily or naturally to most of us, so it requires discipline to enter into it. It is about rightly seeing who we are. An attitude of humility helps us to put God first, others second, and ourselves in last place-- thereby truly submitting to God or someone else.

The people we defer to might be our parents or our boss. This is not saying give in to bullies, but only that we refuse to trample on others because we want something.

What it is not: humility is not about putting yourself down. It is not about groveling in your sin or self-flagellation. It is not selflessness or contempt for yourself. You are made in God's image. There should never be contempt for that!

For all those who exalt themselves will be humbled, and those who humble themselves will be exalted. Jesus Luke 14:11 Niv

Humble Service

———— ...

In the Bible, humble service is so important that it is declared the overarching way that all natural talents and spiritual gifts are acted out. Service done in secret is recommended as the best way to offer service to others. That keeps us humble - if no one knows we did a thing, we can't be outwardly proud of it!

Remember when Jesus knelt down in front of Peter and washed his feet? He was trying to show Peter the gift of humility, through which we serve but also confess that we, too, are in need of grace.

We are constantly reminded by the world to care for ourselves. This self-care can be a healthy practice. But it can become self-serving. So how do we practice self-care and at the same time show humility in our daily lives?

I believe that both are possible. I was taught, and maybe you were too, that we put Jesus first, Others second, Yourself third. The acronym spells JOY. But I am not advocating ignoring your own need. It's not so joyous when a lifetime of always putting yourself last and never attending to your own needs results in pain, chronic illness, and exhaustion.

Taking care of ourselves, particularly getting enough food and rest, helps keep us strong so that we have the ability to put others first. We are still humble; we're just well-rested!

Humility Worksheet

01 Recognize that becoming humble is the foundation that will lead you to all the other godly virtues. Without humility, we could not understand that we need God. It is only by the spirit of God working inside of us that we can see ourselves for who we truly are.

02 Meditate on one of these verses daily. You can keep track on page 35

- ➲ Romans 12:3

- ➲ Matthew 11:29

- ➲ Matthew 18:4.

- ➲ Philippians 2:1-11

- ➲ 2 Chronicles 7:14

- ➲ John 15:5

03 Consider a service that you can do for someone in secret. This must not be ever found out or hinted at by you or those around you. Write it down and determine how you are going to carry it out. Do it this week.

04 Practicing humility often makes us more aware of the joy of living. Sometimes it even gives us confidence. Think of ways you can work on humility on a regular basis. This list may help.

Practice Humility

Below are a few practices to help remind us to live from a place of humility. Because today's world is so self-centered, it's easy to become that way. Tuning into these practices will help you re-center yourself into humbleness.

Meditate on the greatness of God. When we truly submit to the One Who Is All That Is Holy, we realize that everything about us is from him and we have no control over anything in this world.

Be gracious. Ephesians 4:29 says, "Do not let any unwholesome talk come out of your mouths, but only what is helpful for building others up according to their needs, that it may benefit those who listen." Is what you say building others up, or do you spend a lot of time in putdowns and gossip? Make a decision to only say things that will build others up.

Serve. Whenever you serve anyone in any way, you are building up the kingdom of God. Try to find someone every day that you can serve. This could be anything from bringing a cup of coffee to providing money to someone in need. You might find a senior who needs a ride someplace. Better yet, find a way to serve in secret, and never let anyone know!

Submit to all authority. This is difficult in today's world, because we believe strongly in individualism. But we have many authorities in our lives – our pastor, teachers, and superiors on the job. The President of the country is also an authority to whom we should submit.

Create a lowly place. Remember when Jesus said that if you go to your friend's table, you should sit in the lowest place of importance? Often, what we strive for is recognition when we need to strive for is honoring others. Look for the lowly place, and go there.

Bible Verses About Humility

MONDAY	TUESDAY

WEDNESDAY	THURSDAY

FRIDAY	SATURDAY

Meditation as a Spiritual Practice

——————— ...

I used to think that meditation was something related to Eastern religion. I'm not sure why; the Bible speaks to us about meditation, as you see in Psalm 19.

Maybe you felt the same way. What I have learned is that meditation is safe as a Christian practice when we are aligned with God, prayer, and Scripture. It is when we delve into other religions that it becomes an unsafe, unholy place.

In Christian meditation, we think deliberately about something or someone, so that we can better understand the truth. It is a way of contemplating, reflecting, or pondering. During meditation we can come into the presence of God.

> May the words of my mouth and the meditation of my heart be pleasing in your sight, Lord, my Rock and my Redeemer. Jesus Psalm 19:14

Meditation runs counter to a hurried culture like ours. We skim the surface of webpages – it is said that we spend less than 3 seconds deciding whether we want to be there before we click away. We multitask as much as possible, and we look up to those who speed read.

So entering into a meditative state may seem strange to us first. In meditation, you teach your mind to stay focused, centered on one thing. This could be a Scripture verse, a chapter of the Bible, or simply God's creation. It could be a reading (outside of the Bible) or the character of God. You mull over it, ruminate on it, think on it deeply.

As an example, let's look at a Scripture verse: Joshua 1:8.

Keep this Book of the Law always on your lips; meditate on it day and night, so that you may be careful to do everything written in it . Then you will be prosperous and successful.

To meditate on a verse, you may first want to read it several times over, or write it out on a card for reference. This one is straightforward, but if there were unclear parts those could be re-read. Because this verse is from the Old Testament, it is important to look for laws or commands. The command we see here is *Keep this always on your lips*. We do not stop to evaluate ourselves at this moment, since the focus of our meditation is the verse. Rather, we look for how we can obey the command going forward, how we can incorporate it into our daily lives.

At the end of meditation, you may be drawn to pray, praise God, or confess some sin that has been brought to mind.

Use the next two pages to record your meditation experience.

Meditation Worksheet

Meditation helps you have "God eyes" for seeing His world, and it helps use your own inner quiet to develop awareness of Him.

To get started, you do not need any tools unless you are choosing a Scripture verse to work from. Find a place that is distraction free and quiet.

Meditation is the activity of calling to mind, and thinking over, and dwelling on, and applying to oneself, the various things that one knows about the works and ways and purposes and promises of God.
J.I. Packer, *Knowing God*[4].

01	Begin by looking closely at your verse, or at the world around you. Just look and listen.

4   (Downers Grove, IL, InterVarsity, 1973), 23.

02 If you wish, write down questions or comments that come to mind. Use the next page. You may find that one word or phrase seems to be the most important one, the one that keeps resurfacing. Focus more deeply on that one.

03 When your mind wanders, gently return it to the Word (if using) or to the focus phrase you selected.

04 You will most likely move into praise. This is the Holy Spirit leading you exactly where you should go. Don't fight it! Just praise God.

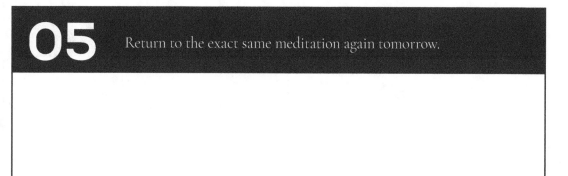

05 Return to the exact same meditation again tomorrow.

My Thoughts On Meditation

MONDAY	TUESDAY

WEDNESDAY	THURSDAY

FRIDAY	SATURDAY

Prayer Walking as a Spiritual Practice

———— ...

Prayer walking is a way of praying on location. There are a couple of different ways that people practice prayer walking - some treating it as exercise plus prayer -but the second type of prayer walk, that of intercessory prayer, is going to be our focus.

In intercessory prayer, you practice on-site prayers while using your senses to gather information about the area. Say you're going to pray for your neighborhood, so you walk around the block as you pray for each family. As you walk, you smell hamburgers on the grill, and see some trees beginning to lose their leaves. You watch some children playing ball in their yard. All five senses come together when prayer walking. You will see, hear, smell, and perhaps taste and touch to understand the prayer needs better.

Sometimes prayer walking is done in groups or as a church, and sometimes it is practiced alone. You are praying in the place that you believe God will answer.

We are commanded to "pray without ceasing" (1 Thessalonians 5:17). So, since walking is something we already do, praying while walking seems a natural way to celebrate this verse.

> 66
> ————
> I am God Almighty; walk before me, and be blameless.
> ~ Genesis 17:1

Did You Know?

Be very aware that as you walk, Satan becomes angry. He has blinded the minds of people so they do not understand what you're doing – and he wants to keep them in the dark. In a sense, you walk humanly alone, but you do it with God! Call on him and praise him for his work in the area you've chosen.

Prepare to Prayer Walk

Prayer walking can be effective and powerful when you plan for it.

01	A prayer walk can be about the area's concerns, or about your own. If you are praying for the place, God will bring the concerns to mind while you are walking.

If the prayer walk is for your own prayers, you might consider the following 3 elements of worship. Which of these will you use today in your first prayer walk?

- ➲ Praise

- ➲ Thanksgiving

- ➲ Repentance

02	Decide how long your walk will be.

03 Decide whether you are going to walk alone or walk with a partner, or as part of a church group.

04 Plan your route.

05 When you walk, walk before the throne of God with an attitude of worship. Magnify the Lord, from where you are.

A Week of Walking Worksheet

Some Ideas For Each Walk

...

01	Pray aloud or pray silently as you go. You may not be walking in order to meet people, but if you interact with anyone, make it an opportunity to offer a blessing. Allow God to use you for practical act of love or kindness.
02	Try prayer walking with Scripture. Scripture is God breathed, and he loves to bless it. If you cannot call Scripture to memory, carry a small Bible or some note cards. You could create a theme for your daily walks.
03	Spend one of your prayer walking days in silence, listening for God's Spirit to speak to you. (John 14:13-14)

Record any insights God gives you as a result of your prayer walk. Be sure to write them down right away. You might even carry a small notebook in your pocket.

After a week spent prayer walking, evaluate what has happened. Do you need to change your route? Change the structure of your prayers? Did you learn anything? Were you able to bless or uplift someone?

I found a nice prayer walking guide for groups here,

- ➲ https://lovekc.net/neighbor-fieldguide/prayerwalking-yourneighborhood/

and a story of a prayer walker here.

- ➲ https://everycampus.com/wp-content/uploads/2020/03/EveryCampus_ prayerwalkguide.pdf

Going Deeper

• • •

The entire Spiritual Practices section has been a difficult lesson, hasn't it? You've "gone deeper" already! In order to go even more in-depth, consider continuing on with the spiritual discipline you've already worked on. Spend another week or month on it. Work on it until you really own it, until it has become part of your daily ritual and you practice it with ease.

If it will not be over whelming doing both at the same time, try some of the"Spiritual Discipline" resources at the end of this book.

To Do and To Be

————— ...

As you lace up your sneakers, being newly strong in the Lord, you may be asking, "What now? What can I do?" Remember that being part of God's plan is not about a checklist of action items. Rather, it flows from our character; from who we are; not from how much we got done in one day. The truths you have absorbed so far must be applied to your life in order for it to be effective. You are engaged with the secular world day in and day out. This gives you continual opportunities for stretching yourself, for using your faith on all levels rather than compartmentalizing it into aSunday/Wednesday pattern.

Journaling the Journey

Keeping a journal, if you never have, may seem like a waste of time at first. Some people seemafraid of keeping a journal, perhaps because of a preconceived notion about what it means.They might even be afraid someone will see their private thoughts written down. Besides,we're all way too busy for that.

But journaling is about self-care. It is good over the long run because it helps you see how far you have come over time. Journaling is a great habit for tracking spiritual growth.

Journaling also helps you see patterns in your own

Write down the revelation and make it plain on tablets.
Habakkuk 2:2, Niv

behavior or responses. For example, if you tend to hold in your feelings until you blow up, journaling, may help you see the beginning part of a problem so that you can address it. Journaling creates an internal map of where you wantto go, both spiritually and emotionally.

Journaling can help us:

- ➲ express feelings
- ➲ clarify a situation
- ➲ work through problems
- ➲ record memories

Did you keep a diary when you were young? I kept a diary every year. I faithfully jotted down everything I had done in my day. But how I wish it had been a journal! Where a diary is a place you record what you did, a journal is a place where you muse and record the "so what." In a journal you figure out the meaning behind your actions, words, or feelings and write them down.

The spiritual journal goes one step further than a diary, because it is a place where you record thoughts, feelings, and ideas related to spirituality. These can be referred to later, helping people look back and see their progress.

Writing is helpful whether you are feeling especially close to God, or whether you are going through difficulties. Writing helps you remember your connection to God and others. It often assists in clarifying what is going on in your heart or your head. Writing helps us focus, so we can be specific about our prayers.

Many people feel it is important to buy a special notebook for spiritual journaling, but that is not necessary. You can use one you already have. A spiral notebook, moleskin, or leather. A handmade notebook. One that fits in your purse or pocket. The choice is yours.

Prepare to Journal

Before starting a journal, there are a few considerations for the layout.

01

Will you proceed in order, or randomly?

Will you date the pages?

Do you need to prep pages (for artwork) like using gesso or paint prior to journaling? If so perhaps work on 2-3 pages ahead of time. Lay wax paper between them while they dry.

02

Is this Journal going to be for a single topic , like gratefulness, or is it going to contain all your thoughts?

03 Plan or schedule journaling time into your day. . Usually 20 minutes is sufficient. What is important is not the amount of time, but the fact that you spend some time every day with the Lord, the regularity of the schedule.

04 Journaling is not about good handwriting, clear thoughts, or grammatically, correct sentences. Rather, in journaling we write freely and quickly. Don't tryt o process the thoughts; just write it down or type it. This gives way to a free flow of thinking, which in turn puts deeper thoughts onto your pages than those you might filter or edit.

Starting the Journal

A few ideas to get a blank page started:

- ➲ Sermon notes

- ➲ Bible verses

- ➲ Things that have been a blessing

- ➲ Gratitude

- ➲ Quotes

- ➲ If you practice a 'word of the year,' journal about using that word

- ➲ Events that happen, and how you felt about them

- ➲ Pictures-either photographs or sketches of something beautiful

- ➲ Art you create as you think on a particular Bible verse

- ➲ Summaries-a summary of the day, week, or month

- ➲ an ongoing conversation with God

Know Scripture

We already covered Scripture study as a Spiritual Practice, but that may not be the one you selected for the week. Besides, this chapter covers Bible study differently. In this unit I am interested in getting Scripture in front of you more than once a day . What I mean is that there are so many of us who take out our Scriptures (at some ungodly hour of the morning,might I add!) ...

We spend ten minutes in it and put it away for the rest of the day. You might say, at least I managed to get to it -and give yourself a pat on the back. And you are correct; good for you!

Impress them on your children. Talk about them when you sit at home and when you walk along the road, when you lie down and when you get up.
Deuteronomy 6:7

The point of having Scripture in front of us each day is to keep it in the forefront of our minds, and you will if you "get to it" daily.

So I want to change it up a little by asking you to receive Scripture in more than one format. This is a chance for you to get creative. You can use Scripture cards, a scrapbook of Scriptures, you can keep a Bible open on your desk at work as well as the home, or one of a million more things. A popular way is to create beautiful wall décor with a verse on it.

The point is to

- ⮑ Get Scripture where you will see it and

- ⮑ Think about it as often as possible.

Are there Scriptures you have memorized? Most of us know at least a few. I've assigned myself to write down the ones that I know into one notebook so that I can (at last!) count them up. However, I'm not finished yet so I can't tell you how many that is.

If memorization is something you would like to work on, perhaps memory verses could become part of your daily routine. I made cute little paper holders for my cards, one for the Already Memorized and one for To Be Memorized. Each day, I pull out a card and work on it. These live on my dresser so that there's no opportunity to skip over them.

But memorization does not have to be a part of this unit. If it fills you with dread, don't do it! I have every confidence that you will eventually memorize some verses accidentally. That does not have to be your focus here.

This video may help: How and Why We Study Scriptures , 28 minutes. You will need to enter this password to view the video: biblestudy. Th is video may help: How and Why We Study Scriptures , 28 minutes. https://youtu.be/InEnXle5vuQ

Let's fill out a simple worksheet so that you can create your own Get-In-the-Scripture plan without my interference or help. Please print the pages "Know Scripture."

Know Scripture

1. Do you already have a daily Bible reading session? Yes no

2. My best way to get a second look at the Bible each day is: (choose one or more)

    a. written plan
    b. by having one open in an accessible area
    c. by using memory cards
    d. through a devotional book
    e. through a Bible plan on my smartphone
    f. through a website on the computer
    g. Just open the Bible

(if you answered no to question one, then in question 2 and forward we are still working on getting you into the Bible once a day. That's fine! Just go with it)

3. From #2 above, write the steps you must take in order to complete that task. Example: you chose (c) through a devotional book. Now you must visit Amazon, select a devotional, and purchase it. Or your steps might be to call a friend, get a book recommendation, and go to the bookstore.

4. Complete the steps in #3.

Notes

Going Deeper

...

Scripture reading is for a lifetime! Donald Whitney said, "No spiritual discipline is more important than the intake of God's word. Nothing can substitute for it. There simply is no healthy Christian life apart from a diet of the milk and meat of Scripture." [5]

---

5   Whitney, D. S. (2014). Spiritual Disciplines for the Christian Life. United States: NavPress., p.22.

To Do and To Be

Oh, my sweet friend. I almost feel that I should leave this section blank, because we both know that if you're in your Bible at all, the Living, Breathing Word is speaking to your heart. It speaks louder, and clearer, and more perfectly than I ever could!

It takes more than one month to make a habit. Let's give it six weeks just to be safe, shall we? So for the next six weeks, can you commit to reading scripture AND the second choice you made on the worksheet above? Take a look at your calendar to see when you might get started.

Let's say you chose memorization. How many verses are you going to memorize? You might have chosen one verse per week. Prepare to begin by writing them out, or printing the cards.

Note the six weeks on your calendar that you're going to practice this habit. When the day comes, begin.

Listen With Your Heart

Listening to God is a funny thing, if you've never done it. Rather than listening with ears while multitasking like we usually do, listening to God requires that we engage the heart. It's a way of hearing that is quieter, more secret and more sacred than anything we have ever done. It is more about personal relationship than any other spiritual practice that we do. It is simply a way of loving God, much as we listened and obeyed our earthly father because we loved and respected him.

There are many reasons why we may refuse to hear it. We may feel unworthy of such an unconditional

> I will instruct you and teach you in the way you should go; I will guide you with my eye.
> Psalm 32:8

promise, or we feel that a sovereign God would never speak to someone as ordinary as "me." We might simply not take the time to listen.

What kind of listener are you? Some listeners wait through the week expectantly for the voice of God. As soon as they hear something, they jot it down or turn over in their mind: How can I practice this? What does he want me to do next?

Other listeners are more passive. They're the ones who hear the sermon, enjoy the message, but make no plans to apply it. As you can guess, these are not the listeners who will usually respond to the voice of God.

Most of us fall somewhere in between.

Make plans to be the purposeful type of listener.

Listening – Why We Listen

01 By listening with the heart, we become teachable and open to the leading of God. In order to listen with the heart, we might pray, "Lord, here I am. Please help me to listen." We may do this several times throughout the day in order to remember to listen for his voice.

02 We listen to God in order to know His specific plan for our lives. We know from the Bible that his will is for us to serve him. However, we don't know the specifics of that servanthood. Where will we work? Whom will we marry? Should we have children? These are all things that God needs to help us with individually. Most of us make a decision, like a certain career, then we desperately want God to bless that decision. It might be best to ask first, then make the choice. Quiet listening will usually be the key to finding the answer.

03 Along the same line, we are each called to "build and edify" the church, but we might not be clear on our specific calling. This is where we must depend on hearing from God.

Plan to hear the voice of God.

Listening – How We Listen

When listening to God, we open ourselves up to every possibility that surrounds us. We may hear his voice in the voice of another human being who speaks to us, be it a friend or a counselor. We may hear it through the sound of the birds singing, a rushing waterfall, or by watching a situation unfold. I seem to hear him a lot in the shower. God speaks to us in manyways, and we must realize that we are always in his presence. It is always possible to hear the voice of God.

Following are a few hints for when you are trying to hear God's voice.

Look for Him in others.

The voice that we hear is that of the Holy Spirit, which lives within us - even when it is coming from the mouth of a friend or pastor. He nudges our spirit through the other person, or sometimes we say he impresses it upon our heart. This is how God speaks to us.

Write it down.

It doesn't have to be well-written or even complete sentences, but jot down exactly what you heard - especially if it seems to be in your own voice. Use it to think over what you (think you) heard, or share with others who can help you decide if it was from God.

> **Verify.**
>
> The leading of the Holy Spirit will always line up with God's word. In fact, he often brings Scripture to mind just as he is telling us what our next step is going to be.

- ⮞ Always be on the alert for His voice.

- ⮞ Look for validation in Scripture .

Listening – Does it Make Sense?

You may wonder what will happen if the thing you hear in your heart does not seem to make common sense. In these cases, you can bet that his leading will come to you in several different avenues. It didn't make common sense for Noah to take 120 years building a boat – when it never rained! It didn't make sense for Joshua to march around the city of Jericho 7 times. But God gave special revelation to these people so that they would understand their instructions in a clear way. So when you have really big, exciting assignments from God, be assured that he will tell you in several ways that it is the right thing to do.

Often you will wonder whether the 'will' you are answering is your own or God's, or even the devil's. This is a very valid question, because we can want things badly enough to tell ourselves that we're really hearing from God when we're not.

If you are not sure you've truly heard from God – wait. While waiting, check Scripture for validation and consider whether this answer brings peace to your heart. Validation can come from a trusted friend, your prayer partner, or your pastor. It may come by hearing the same thing spoken aloud from people who know you. You may see or hear a "sign" and realize it's part of the same divine plan the Lord spoke to you about.

For me, the end validation often comes in threes. Here's an example.

A Personal Story

...

I hope you don't mind if I get a little personal here. See, I wanted really badly to move to Florida. Even as a child I said, "I want to wake up to the sound of the ocean." But "life" happened, and I pushed that dream aside.

When we married in 2008, my husband Mickey and I lived in land-locked Tennessee, but we often traveled to Florida. Oh, I wanted so badly to move there! His family lived there; shouldn't we live there, too?

One time when driving through Florida in the pouring rain, I realized my fibromyalgia was not acting up. Back home, rain meant a lot of stiffness, pain, and possibly going to bed. I mentioned it to Mickey and asked, "Could we move here?"

His natural response to anything is "no." So I was surprised when he came back to me the next day (after the initial no) and said we could consider it. "We work for ourselves, we can move our businesses," he said. **That's one.**

Well, guess who hadn't prayed about it? But as we prayed, we received a lot of validation. One friend said we needed to get away and form our own memories. **(That's two)**

Others felt Mickey's business would thrive in a new location. **(That's three plus)**

As I created my art journal page about it, I felt overwhelming peace. That was the ultimate **confirmation.**

We realized this was the best plan. Eight years later, we're still thrilled to live in Florida.

Decide Who's in Charge

God promises his guidance to people who have already surrendered to his word. In advance, we have agreed to do it – even before we know what "it" is. I remember one woman said she promised to always say "okay" to her husband, no matter how bad she thought his request was. They were a missionary family, and a lot of his requests centered around moving. I'm not sure how easily I would be able to say "okay" to constant moves, often to remote locations in other countries!

Always ending prayers with, "not my will, but yours" (and meaning it) assures us that we are emptying ourselves in order to be refilled with the will of the father

When we live surrendered, we live in God's will.

In Lesson 4, we talked about God's answer being yes, no, or not right now. When considering whether an action is based on the will of God, and wondering if that's his voice in your heart, the best thing is to **wait.**

Waiting on the Lord is a common practice in Scripture. It means that we wait until we are absolutely sure that we are taking the right action before we do so. No matter how big or small the request is - prayerfully wait. Waiting is the mature response to being unsure. You cannot go wrong. Then when you hear the quiet voice telling you the way to walk, you'll be certain of where you're going next.

Let's take a look at some people in Scripture who waited.

Abraham	waited on a son. Genesis 12 21, Romans 4:18 25.
Jacob	waited for Rebecca. Genesis 29:1 30.
David	waited to become King. (1 Samuel 16 he was revealed as the choice)
Mary, mother of Jesus	waited 30 years for her son to be the Messiah. Luke 1:31 33
Jesus	waited for God's voice before he could start his ministry. Matthew 3:17, Matthew 17:5.

Who else waited in the Bible? Study one or more characters carefully. What did they do while they waited?

Prayerfully wait.

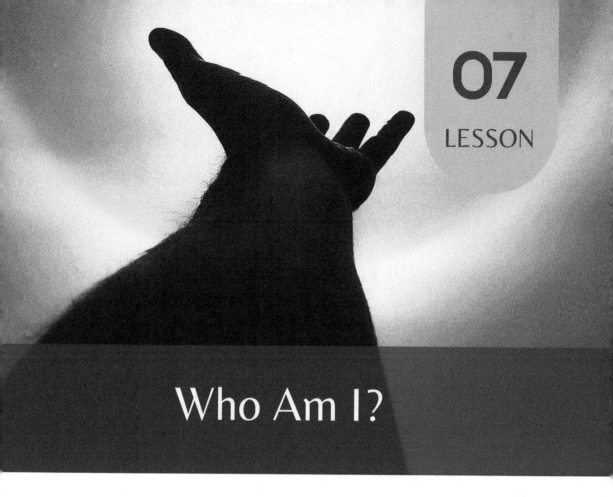

Who Am I?

I wanted to call this Lesson "Walk the Walk" and talk about how to keep all aspects of our lives in tune with God's leading. Uh, yeah. Can anyone say **encyclopedia?**

So that one went into the maybe, someday pile. Instead, I'd like to talk to you about who you are, and more importantly who you are in Christ.

When we walk with God we do our best, then we fail, we ask for forgiveness, and we restart. It's a cycle. Everybody does it.

> I am complete in Him Who is the head over all rule and authority— of every angelic and earthly power
> Colossians 2:10

In fact the Israelites as a nation practiced the Sin Cycle; throughout the Old Testament you can see God withholding blessings until they (once again) repented and started anew. We are no different.

So we will not be perfect, at least on this earth. The question then becomes: When things are bad, when the sky seems to be falling, when catastrophe strikes, when I lose my job/spouse/child/car – what do I do first?

If you answered 'pray,' you are far ahead of the game. Many of us do not pray. Some turn away from God, either deliberately or subconsciously. Some blame God for their misfortune. Some simply sink into deep depression. Only a few actually reach for God.

But that is the second half of our equation. First we need to address the first half. So – who are you?

Please answer below.

Who I Am In Christ

In asking this question, I'm not asking you to tell me about your job, family, or hobbies. If you asked me about those, I would say: Christian writer, wife, mom, pet lover, etc.

Those things do not describe my character. They are good descriptive phrases, and good answers for small talk with a new acquaintance. Instead, let's answer these questions:

- ➲ Who are you when you see a neighbor struggling to carry in the groceries?

- ➲ Who are you when an annoying person runs up to you at church wanting a hug?

- ➲ Who are you when you drop your favorite collectable and break it?

Jot a few thoughts here

Goodness

———— ...

Although God wants us to be 'good,' that is not the top priority on His list. When we start following rules and working for goodness, we forget to work toward holiness and humility. In fact, striving to be good can get in the way of our walk with God. He requires only that we come to Him as we are. He doesn't want us to wait until we've become good enough!

So our goal is not to be good. I know you've probably internalized the idea of "being good," as did I. Our parents helped us with that. But now we need to re-think it. We don't need to have goodness as a goal anymore. Instead we need **holiness** and **humility.**

What did Jesus say were the most important goals? "To love God with all your heart, soul and mind, and love your neighbor as yourself." (paraphrase from Matthew 22)

He didn't say be good. He didn't say be anything. He said do. An action word. Love. Go and love God. Go and love your neighbor. Love is the greatest gift God gave us. Love is the best fruit from the Holy Spirit.

So who is our neighbor? I define "neighbor" as anyone within proximity, for whom I can brighten the day. That might seem broad, but:

- ➲ If I'm in the front yard, my neighbor is the guy across the street.

- ➲ If I'm in the grocery store, my neighbor is the person in my aisle or in my line.

- ➲ If I'm at church, my neighbor is the entire church family plus the visitors.

See? Neighbors are simply the people around us. Now, the things we're going to do for them are "good" but they need to spring from love. It is not what we do—those good things!—it is what's in our hearts as we do them.

Some of you who are reading this are a lot better than I am at doing for others. I see many people doing small favors that I don't think of doing. I seem to have missed that gene. I'm not pleased about it (you want to be one of the kindest women, right?) but there we are.

The Lord actually told me to work on loving others a few years ago, and it brought about a huge change. I learned that when your action is from the heart, it is more joyful to you. Trying to look at people the way Jesus sees them, and trying to love them has been one of the most challenging things God has ever put me through. But with that, I have been able to love better (in fact I think that is exactly what He said to me: Love better), and I experience more joy than ever before.

For one thing, because I am trying to practice loving others, I'm looking at every single person – not the pretty ones or the fun ones or my favorites. I'm looking at the dirty, the unkempt, the one with the overly loud voice, the one who sits alone. And I'm thinking, Jesus loves her; how can I love her?

And as soon as I figure out how to love that person, I put it into action. One friend pointed out that your smile at someone in a grocery line might be the only smile a person gets all day. I try to smile or say something kind to people around me. Often I come across someone who simply needs a listening ear. I listen attentively and take care not to interrupt. I never knew before this how many people are dying for someone to hear what they have to say.

What I enjoy doing for others:

Some other ideas are:

- ⮥ Give money or material items to meet a need.

- ⮥ Divide your plants in order to have one ready to give away.

- ⮥ Handmake a gift just to bring pleasure. One person was startled when I made her a simple necklace. "I can't think of how long it's been since anybody gave me a present, much less made it," she said.

Those are just a few examples to get you thinking about loving people. Giving to people out of love creates joy— in both of you. Love your neighbor. Love. Go and truly love.

Oh and being "good?" That naturally happens while we're loving. There is no need to think on it anymore. What a relief.

Use this page to brainstorm new ways you might do good things for others. Will you do it in secret, or not?

Who in your life could really use a lift right now? How could you make that happen?

Record experience and be ready to share with the group.

Humility

Humility (NOUN) The quality or condition of being humble; modest opinion or estimate of one's own importance, rank, etc.

Humility is an elusive thing. As an observer, you can find people who believe they are humble when in fact they are anything but. Arrogance seeps from their very pores. You almost can't stand to meet their bragging eyes. On the flip side, ancient monks, who probably live the humblest lives of all, constantly berated themselves for their lack of humility! Surely there is a healthy middle ground.

Humble yourselves before the Lord, and he will exalt you.
James 4:10

You may have chosen humility as one of your spiritual discipline practices in Lesson 2. If that's the case, feel free to move on to the next section.

The rest of us will think for a time on humility. I find it impossible to teach. Perhaps leading by example is a better choice. Remember when you noticed that guy at church suppers, who always seemed to herd everyone into the line - then ended up last? Don't you think he was hungry? Yet he placed himself at the back of the line. That's humble.

Or maybe your grandmother was like mine, staying on her feet all day in the kitchen, constantly bringing food and drink to the crowd that sat at the table. Now that I'm an adult and my grandmother is long gone, I realize how tired she must have been some days. I also wonder why more adults didn't help serve! But that's for another day.

Practice Humility

Below are a few practices to help remind us to live from a place of humility. Because today's world is so self-centered, it's easy to become that way. Tuning into these practices will help you re-center yourself into humbleness.

- ➲ **Meditate on the greatness of God.** When we truly submit to the One Who Is All That Is Holy, we realize that everything about us is from him and we have no control over anything in this world.

- ➲ **Be gracious.** Ephesians 4:29 says, "Do not let any unwholesome talk come out of your mouths, but only what is helpful for building others up according to their needs, that it may benefit those who listen." Is what you say building others up, or do you spend a lot of time in putdowns and gossip? Make a decision to only say things that will build others up.

- ➲ **Serve.** Whenever you serve anyone in any way, you are building up the kingdom of God. Try to find someone every day that you can serve. This could be anything from bringing a cup of coffee to providing money to someone in need. You might find a senior who needs a ride someplace. Better yet, find a way to serve in secret, and never let anyone know!

- ➲ **Submit to all authority**. This is difficult in today's world, because we believe strongly in individualism. But we have many authorities in our lives – our pastor, teachers, and superiors on the job. The President of the country is also an authority to whom we should submit.

⮑ **Create a lowly place**. Remember when Jesus said that if you go to your friend's table, you should sit in the lowest place of importance? Often, what we strive for is recognition when we need to strive for is honoring others. Look for the lowly place, and go there.

Exercise: Humility

· · ·

Pride comes to us naturally, and yet your mother probably always told you that pride also goes before a fall (Proverbs 16:18). It is only by living as a conduit for God's service that we become humble.

⮑ Please read:

1 Peter 3:8-17

James 4

⮑ This section on humility resonates with me. (circle) YES NO

⮑ I plan to put the following into practice this week:

Holiness

For it is written: "Be holy, because I am holy." ~ 1 Peter 1:16

Many people find that this verse fills them with dread. It is an impossible, unattainable goal. Only God is truly holy, and yet we strive for holiness ourselves. How can we even think that our sinful, lowly selves could somehow become holy?

Let's look at it differently. Think about your family and the things you inherited from them: blue eyes, brown hair, your height, etc. My mother could say, "You will be short because I am short." My father could say, "You will have dark hair because I have dark hair." In the same manner, God says, "Be holy because I am holy."

Holiness is part of the inheritance package. It is our father's gift to us.

Holiness is not about our condemned state. I know we spend a lot of time talking and thinking about our notholy selves, how shattered and damaged and integrity-less we are. Instead, maybe it's time to focus on the promise God made that we will be holy, and His grace in making us that way. Maybe the sentence above would be clearer like this:

"Because your Father is holy, be assured that you are already on your way to holiness."

Doesn't that feel better than some elusive goal?

We already are on the way to holiness because the Holy Spirit dwells inside us. The Holy Spirit wants to bring each of us to our fully sanctified, best self. He wants to put you together spiritually, emotionally and physically, right now.

To achieve holiness, we must allow the Holy Spirit to help us reach sanctification (holiness). Billy Graham said, "Do not ask Him to help you as you would a servant. Ask Him to come in and do it all. Ask Him to take over in your life." Graham, Billy, Peace With God: the Secret of Happiness, Thomas Nelson, 1953. P.208.

> And I have been a constant example of how you can help those in need by working hard
> Acts 20:35

Please watch this video on holiness (5 minutes). https://youtu.be/_mU2xVoVZKs

To find holiness, we must look to God and see how His holiness is exhibited. This can be seen most readily in the person of Jesus Christ. The apostle Paul suggested that we imitate Christ (1 Thessalonians 1 &2). Imitation in this case refers to both the outward example and the inward attitude. In another letter, he admonished the elders,

Paul believed strongly in following by example, and that others would then follow you—thereby creating a chain of holy behavior.

We use the word holiness in titles, in speech, and in song. What does holiness mean to you?

Who You are in Christ, cont'd

How has this lesson changed your view of holiness?

In what way can you increase holiness in your life, today?

The sections above have helped you determine who you are. As Christians, our identity is not "I am a mother and a computer programmer." It is seen through the god-lens. Only in Him can we see ourselves wholly and truthfully. So now we're back to that question:

Who are you in Christ?

> Write a few thoughts about your Christ identity here

In the previous section, we touched on imitating Christ. In order to imitate, we must truly know who we are dealing with. Did you ever imitate a sibling when you were young? You had to really know your brother's walk in order to walk like him. You had to really know your sister's speech patterns to pretend to be her on the telephone. In the same way, we must really know Christ to imitate His way of being and doing.

On a scale of 1-10, how well do you know Christ? 0 1 2 3 4 5 6 7 8 9 10

> What steps can you take to get to know Him better today?

We can grow and change in Christ, no matter how long we've been a Christian. That is part of the promise of sanctification—that we continue to grow in grace of Jesus our Lord and Savior. Imitating Christ is one step in that pattern.

When we walk with God, we walk in agreement with Him. Walking with God means going:

In the same direction. We must learn what that direction is (hint: It always leads toward holiness, not away from it).

In step. When you walk with someone, it is always a comfort to share the same walking pattern: steps, stride length, footfalls in rhythm. It is no different with God. We find the rhythm He wants us to use, and walk that way.

Notes

Conclusion

I wrote this guide as a way to lead people just one step closer to God. Are you feeling it now? If so – celebrate a little bit! If you're not, would you please send a quick note and let me know where I failed you? That would help me a lot.

In each section, we talked about how you would

- ➲ Find a sacred space

- ➲ Develop a routine for prayer

Try a discipline you haven't tried before

- ➲   Begin to journal the journey

- ➲   Listen with your heart

- ➲   Get the Word in front of you more than once a day

- ➲   Find practical ways to practice love, holiness, and humility

Please examine the list carefully. If you skipped over any part, please go back and complete it now. If you choose not to, of course, that's okay. This is your journey.

As you continue to practice each of these steps, you will lay the brick-by-brick foundation for a steady, full, and fruitful life in the Spirit. I urge you to keep this manuscript in a safe place and come back to it; you can repeat the steps regularly and gain even more understanding each time.

My prayer for you is that you will continue to walk forward with Jesus as your guide.

I pray that you always seek his guidance, and hear his voice above the noise of the world.

I pray that your family will draw strength from you, and will not falter nor succumb to the enemy who lurks.

I pray that you will hide the Word in your heart and draw on its comfort, wisdom, and guidance daily.

May you be blessed beyond blessing, beyond words, and beyond your wildest dreams.

Tanya

More Books by This Author

...

- ⇒ The Gouldian Finch handbook
- ⇒ Feeding Finches
- ⇒ Come Back to Jesus and Don't Bring your Blackberry
- ⇒ How to Be Your Own Contractor and Save Thousands on Your New House or Renovation (While Keeping your Day Job)
- ⇒ How to Open an Operate a Financially Successful Construction Company
- ⇒ The Real Estate Developer's Handbook.

Where to find me:

...

- ⇒ TanyaLogan.com
- ⇒ Facebook: https://facebook.com/TanyaLoganAuthor

It is said that an author is only as good as his/her last book review. We literally depend on those reader reviews for our work. Would you mind taking a moment now and leaving a review of this book? You can do it on Amazon, B&N, Apple, or wherever you purchased this copy. Your opinion means a lot to me.

I can't thank you enough for reading the book, and I sincerely hope you found some small nuggets that feel as if they were written just for you.

Resources

Following are some books, videos and podcasts you might find useful.

Books:

...

- ➲ Spiritual Disciplines for the Christian Life, Donald Whitney.

- ➲ The Life You've Always Wanted: Spiritual Disciplines for Ordinary People, John Ortberg.

- ➲ Celebration of Discipline: The Path to Spiritual Growth, Richard Foster.

Podcasts:

———   ...

- ➲ Greg Laurie
- ➲ David Platt
- ➲ Your Daily Prayer
- ➲ Shalom Sistas
- ➲ Rick Warren

Youtube Channels:

———   ...

- ➲ Grace to you (my personal favorite)
- ➲ Desiring God
- ➲ The Anima Series
- ➲ The Gospel Coalition

Bible App:

———   ...

- ➲ Youversion

Printed in the USA
CPSIA information can be obtained
at www.ICGtesting.com
LVHW010147041123
762867LV00042B/357

9 781735 832821